Nearness

Your life in the world is your story.
Write well. Edit often.

~ *Anonymous*

Also, by Leonard Neufeldt

Painting Over Sketches of Anatolia
(Signature Editions, 2015)
How to Beat the Heat in Bodrum
(Alfred Gustav Press, 2010)
The Coat is Thin
(Cascadia Publishing House, 2008)
Before We Were the Land's
(Horsdal & Schubert, 2002) Heritage Award.
Car Failure North of Nîmes
(Black Moss Press, 1994)
Yarrow
(Black Moss Press, 1993)
Raspberrying
(Black Moss Press, 1991) Lambert Prize shortlist.
The Economist: Henry Thoreau and Enterprise
(Oxford Univ. Press, 1989)
The House of Emerson
(Univ. of Nebraska Press, 1982)
Awarded "1983 Best Academic Book," (national).
Christian Gauss Prize, Phi Beta Kappa Society shortlist.
A Way of Walking
(Univ. of New Brunswick Press Fiddlehead Series, 1972)

Nearness

by

Leonard Neufeldt

720 Sixth St., Box # 5
New Westminster, BC
V3L 3C5 CANADA

Title: NEARNESS
Author: Leonard Neufeldt
Cover Design: Candice James
Layout and Editing: Candice James
© 2020 Silver Bow Publishing

ISBN 9781774030745 (softcover)
ISBN 9781774030752 (e-book)

All rights reserved including the right to reproduce or translate this book or any portions thereof, in any form without the permission of the publisher. Except for the use of short passages for review purposes, no part of this book may be reproduced, in part or in whole, or transmitted in any form or by any means, electronically or mechanically, including photocopying, recording, or any information or storage retrieval system without prior permission in writing from the publisher or a license from the Canadian Copyright Collective Agency (Access Copyright). Copyright to all individual poems remains with the author.

Library and Archives Canada Cataloguing in Publication

Title: Nearness / by Leonard Neufeldt.
Names: Neufeldt, Leonard, author.
Description: Poems.
Identifiers: Canadiana (print) 20200173456 | Canadiana (ebook) 20200173472 | ISBN 9781774030745
   (softcover) | ISBN 9781774030752 (ebook)
Classification: LCC PS8577.E758 N43 2020 | DDC C811/.54—dc23

Nearness

for
Bob, Elmer, Elsie, and Larry
and, as always,
for Mera

Nearness

Acknowledgments

My gratitude to editors of the following publications, in which some of these poems appeared:

Antigonish Review: "Immigrant Work"; Canto 8 of "Cantos of Oak"

Cirque: "The Return"

Descant: Cantos 1-4, 6, 7, 9 of "Cantos of Oak"

Event: "Crescent Lake"; "How the World Reflects Itself in Myra, Turkey"; "Time As Distance"

Freefall: "Southward"

Half in the Sun (anthology): "Why Our Town Replaced Silver Maples with Better Trees"

Leaping Clear: "Harrier"; "North of the Assiniboine"

Prairie Fire: "Anniversary of the Lost Boreal Forests"; "Birches of Lake Winnipeg"; "Canto 5 of "Cantos of Oak"; "North of Boreality"; "Words and Tree"

Rhubarb: "Don't Ask"

West Texas Literary Review: "The Yellow Transparent Apple Tree"

Alfred Gustav Press Chapbook Series : Cantos 2-5, 8, 9, 11-16, 18 of "Pacific Cantos"

Nearness

Table of Contents

Immigrant Work ... 11

I   More-Than-Human Nearness ... 13

Crescent Lake ... 15
Harrier ... 16
North of the Assiniboine ... 17
New Year's Day in the Foothills ... 18
Winter Sun in Puget Sound Country ... 20
The Return ... 22
Southward ... 24
Helleborus Niger ... 25
How the World Reflects Itself in Myra, Turkey ... 27
End of the Tourist Season in Bodrum ... 28
The Wall ... 30
Flying into the Namib Desert ... 33
Full Hunter's Moon ... 35
The Vedder River Run ... 36
Steelhead Trout ... 37
October Slugs ... 39
Time as Distance ... 40
Consanguinity ... 42
Hum of Bees ... 43

II   Pacific Cantos ... 45-56

III Trees Partly of Wood ... 57

Anniversary of the Lost Boreal Forests ... 59
North of Boreality ... 60
Why Our Town Replaced Silver Maples with Better Trees ... 62

Graduate Studies ... 65
Ice Storm ... 68
Don't ask ... 70
The Yellow Transparent Apple Tree ... 71
Pink Dogwood ... 73
Birches of Lake Winnipeg ... 75
Words and Tree ... 79

IV Cantos of Oak ... 81 – 96

Author Profile ... 97

Immigrant Work

I walked the quarter-mile rows of vines
on September days opening themselves
to a sky uncertain even then,
a lifetime ago when I left boyhood
too soon for hard labour in the hop yards,
my machete slashing through the heads
of trellised vines and through
the double strings that held them
to the high wire brought down,
my arm tight as the bow
when I would bring the violin
to my chin, ready,
ahead of me the school dropout
twice my size, his long pole
tipped with the metal curl: *wire
coming down* or simply
wire down pisshead

I'm walking a long sentence
between deserted rows which lead
to more rows in the niggling breeze,
the emerald green of feathery flowers,
hardly two alike, nettling my bare arms.
Still too young, even so stalking
perfect strokes among
the sweaty fumblings, a place
where I know more than I should
and imagine what I will learn to be

The harvest still coming at summer's end

Nearness

More-Than-Human Nearness

Nearness

Crescent Lake

Small crossings of dreams
on the windshield
riding down, separating,
seeking something more –
the swerve sudden as the night
narrowing the unstriped road
and bending
an invisible margin of shore

Trees lean our way
in the headlights. And distance?
With only these beams
tracing the start of the next curve,
not even a dark mouth of water.
We see nothing more
than a half-rondure of wipers
edging the rain and the night's real work

How long is a moment of blackness
that will not end?
You sitting up with me

I had imagined the sound
of small streams falling
to the earth out of the night
and on the other side
catspaws of ripples
running shoreward,
spreading themselves
under a mantle of stars

You sitting up, watching –
so much unknown nearness

Harrier

A long whistle echoes
change in the air,
argues nearness
from the valley's far side,
an oncoming
making adjustments
to find you

the already, the moment's burst,
car after car
counting spaces,
rushing them away
as though the world
has to be emptied
like evening,
the absence naked
as the mountains

and the V-shape lifting
from the dead tree,
its glide alone
into the dark

You almost ready
for the suddenness,
for the beauty of desolation,
the day's end
exactly this

North of the Assiniboine

The wheat fields' roll
and roll of dark afterlife
explaining the gold
gone

the air whiter, a change
cottoned like a gathering from sleep,
inside the wind where you stopped
ribbons of first snow, small seizures
busy with their silence
of following each other
across the gravel road
like the eagerness in you
alive to what is on the other side

You fold and refold your map without looking,
and because you wait for the fibrillose tempo
and small feelings in your hands to ease,
the fields grow larger,
a sudden getting-clear-of,
momentary greatness
of blue all the way to the horizon,
to a lone spruce
black against the margin's emptiness,
your readiness to . . .

Say them,
words of winter,
like stammerings of first love
finding themselves –
so simple

New Year's Day in the Foothills

The horses know their way around
hidden ice sheets
but the red-flannel hostler
made sure the stirrups easily detached,
his teeth chattering.
No end to small wind bursts
and surface lurch of snow.
Winter read to the senses,
finding every part of us

So naked the shivers inside our layers
as the horses step through explosions of breath.
We rein in: a wooden tower
poised like an old example of itself,
as if counting the rasps of bare branches
against its grey warp
as an owl, half-way up, head-swivels
for us to see a large roundness of eyes,
the excellent face it makes,
each swivel a separate function
like the tower's creaks, each one
accounting for the previous one
until our face and hands are numb

Slow feather ruffle and then,
its whiteness shrinks again

Nothing here has a plot:
not even the owl
huddled completely inside itself, eyes closing;
not even the tower
concentrating its lack of protection;
not even the wind's work
to lose whatever feeling remains

Nearness

It is not winter's business
to be anything but what it is

Like the clarity of a sheet of frozen water

And the only way back
is the way we came,
reading the signs

Winter Sun in Puget Sound Country

Power-line pylons, like empty altars
above the tide line, yielding to nothing
but the rain and excess of silent-movie grey
darkening in moments of breath
on your eyeglasses

A solitary gull shrieks into the sky's getaway
of lost connections,
a thought left behind without a shadow
four weeks of rain
must be dangerous to someone
and so, what to do with more days coming

Walk the rhythm
of the rain hat's drumming up Peacock Hill
past ladders against gutters,
almost ready to think some things
are permanent in your cul-de-sac,
watching to see if anything has changed,
if anyone hurries

Put on dry clothes.
Say that rain
keeps a person from swallowing
didactic refusals without chewing

Say you're not hungry
and go down to your well-lit room,
turn over the sketch-pad page
and draw a circle,
its centre anywhere,
and let the circle bear south
across the dun of shore
and east through a full range

Nearness

of mountain-blue erasure
to the slightest wisp of smoke
breathing a desolate waywardness
from no apparent place.
A small signature,
an opening for the light

The Return

All this goose-strutting
like revanchist warriors, shofar necks
coaxing head bobs into mutters
almost done with bickering.
But their battle of wills wants it back,
the sodden field that Tundra swans
claimed just days ago,
the Canada geese circling like a gridlock,
a few swans getting through

The sky a bloat of clouds,
the boardwalk a splatter of rain
yet few drops attach themselves to you
as though you're not even here
in the Fraser Valley,
to which you've returned, unsure of why

Perhaps to see for yourself –
the avalanche on the Vedder Mountain Road
a litter of brokenness like the old god of argument,
the spleen of whatever mattered then,
and here by the boardwalk
it's the fullness of cedars,
the empty details of cottonwoods,
the swans' white on the grass still green,
the light rinsed clean
and wetland ripples keeping time with the wind
and with small-winged shadows
bursting down through the sunlit edge
from the clouds' dark rooms,
wing-slap in the chill
beyond the weariness of wonder,
following each other in ragged ellipses
that make the air intimate,

Nearness

the cinnamon teal's kind of rhythm
wary of the earth's pull and the sky
above and behind

Who can say how the need to return
or leave first began?
A need that belongs to itself and you.
This time you won't pretend to know,
the teal gone as suddenly as they came,
the long hunt adjusting somewhere
to another flash of water and field,
the world's curve keeping desire alive,
the rain much more real than it was,
the stutter of swans lifting away
and huddles of geese watching them settle
to feed farther back
as though staying and watching
is how to return,
and you shifting your feet
from the mossy edge
where the boardwalk begins
to circle back

Southward

No need to ask what the sundogs mean.
The notes begin out of the wind-frozen stream
and snow running in a burst
over the charcoal ruffle of the spruce grouse
and the marmot's quick look left and right

Leafless willows mark the way
to the end of the sky's immensity;
to where what's below rises up:
sprouts from inside the earth,
pool of black in the hoof print,
last year's grass splayed into fold lines
of giving way to green,
light gathering shadows and mist
at the end of a watery meadow
where the river begins,
where the alpha wolf stands astride
the double line of the Yellowknife Highway;
he will not move
but mountain silhouettes
drift southward past evening,
their gleams of caution
stalking the night's distance
from the Fraser Canyon to the Pacific
past fogs breathing the emptiness
of new fields;
a long way,
and the stars know it,
and the first light,
the small-leafed dawn,
the song cool in the lungs

Helleborus Niger

February, and you were ready,
checked-in bags sagging with what you left behind.
A well-lit corridor to your plane
after the two-month humdrum in Lycia
with Turkish friends
and their direct, non-stop wish
for comfortable leg room to America,
their words like the straight-line black weave
of power lines through almond blossoms,
a mostly hardened prose of resaying
to the end

CNN International
hesitating at the boarding gate
to listen to the whispers rushing through

But at thirty-eight thousand feet
homecoming wants a list,
and at the top of yours
the hooded shimmers, separate,
sure of themselves and their petals
in praise of another winter
without snow in Gig Harbor,
no matter how cold:
the white spell cast of hellebores,
their respect for the trees' simple emptiness
in front and back
and the dark wash of mulch,
other details cut away
after the frost's first hard intention

You in the window seat
guessing where the sea, the continent

Home

You twist out of your night dreams,
their fickleness of plans,
and find the floor's naked chill,
let it exchange a moment with you
before you step out of the room
and around the suitcases still at the front door

You leave the door open behind

The hellebores' long-stalked leaves
have divided fan-like, a few showing their teeth
when you look closely into the lustrous green
and the flowers clustering their all-colour
no-colour chill of a single joy,
the equity of hellebore white,
bare feet and first morning back

How the World Reflects Itself in Myra, Turkey

> *We cannot look*
> *At what we love without failure*
> Ann Lauterbach, "Mimetic"

Body waves of air
bonded to light
like a narrative of awakening

You do not look into the sun;
you do not look behind the sunrise,
you look aslant, away
to find where you are
in this day's embroidery

Slopes of green
and long shadows open to you
like a morning that matters,
that like you,
is known by all that surrounds it

You look at what you love
as you set out,
down through blood-orange orchards
and cypress spires
into summer

End of the Tourist Season in Bodrum

Billions of notices from the Milky Way,
the lightyears negotiating the stars'
dimming down and the edge to dawn
behind the high ridge silhouette
breathing past outlines
of unroofed windmills
and watch-tower ruins
still encrusted with dark

Below, the Aegean itself again, separate,
and the scented shadow play of the world
begins its mute expenditures
as though this day wants to be
a willing prelude to itself
and to the start of slight sounds
from the Underwater Museum
(closed this year) where shipwrecks
of 2000 years are being pieced
together by those who say they can do it;
those who know how to debrief
watery ghosts even more secretive
than God is supposed to be,
a hands-on gentleness
with a ribcage of sea-bottom wood
and almost weightless working papers

Herodotus, main stayed by vestige
and a pedestal beside the entrance gate,
watches the gain and loss
of an empty life raft adrift
in ribbons of light beyond the marina,
a tiny reckoning in so much open sea,
so much morning

Nearness

There is too much that cannot give back,
the language strange
as a full arc of sky or a statue
ready, it seems, to grow taller,
to shuffle out past its shade,
to look toward the ridge,
watch the sun labour
to engulf a watchtower ruin,
unmoved by time's exit wounds

The marine archeologists work
until sundown

More refugees will drown tonight

The Wall

We've reached the house we rented
with trust as down payment,
the way we trust each other's body
and its narratives.
In the glass wall's wide-angle precision
a mirrored world: the volcano's blue;
poinsettias' flash of red in the radiance of day's end;
long shapes girdling coconut palms
with a hide-and-seek of light.
We turn to study them, the tin wraps at the base
to keep rats' midnight go-betweens at ground level.
The sea floating a cloud-bank horizon

* *

The secrets of the dark darker because
of lamps behind us and the moon
dividing the glass wall and an oceanic night.
Undraped bodies just beyond the glass
glide toward us, stop, the same and not the same,
amused, coming closer, startled as we touch,
the glass almost letting in their shapes.
We touch again, your hand, your scar's small shiver

* *

"The cyclone turned 90 degrees yesterday,
but heavy glass panels properly framed"
(the radio at daybreak) "can withstand
almost any storm if correctly taped,
and if all the outside has been secured."
We've always been reliable housekeepers,
aware of what must be done and when,
even of what we can become better at.
But a glass wall on the Pacific

Nearness

can belie what's here in the gusts'
eager conjugations and what's coming,
a surprise, neither chosen, nor right or wrong.
Soon it will scream contradictions
into the heart of everything, and category one means
what we were sure would never be, is:
the hysterical radio monotone,
a wall shaking out uncertain sighs and thwacks
as clouds scour the sky. The wind's gleam
explodes from lurid corridors of light
shattering the air, the rain sideways,
palms plunging unbraided heads toward us,
throwing their long necks back up
where we want them to stay, fronds
breaking away from themselves, hitting the glass
like frantic birds, the fence levitating
above the grass and sinking back to where it fell,
papaya trees stepping away from their feet,
first one, then the other,
falling, turning over from side to side
on the ground, their fruit smashed
like pumpkins in a zoo cage.
Unrehearsed parts, a one-sided frenzy
of overlapping moments, none having time
to finish. The cabana's whiteness
lifts from its base like a kite,
folds midair into itself as it hurtles our way.
We fall back, watch it darken like a giant hand
etching a comet's tail the full length of the glass
before cartwheeling too explicitly
across the flattened fence

* *

How to begin after terrible dispersal,
the tumult no more, the space between us
and the glass large enough for long pauses

Nearness

remaindered by the storm
as though they should know
a glass house in a cyclone
is not the place for love
to venture out or start over

It's not a question of drawing open the door
of our wants, and it's not the whispers
of a blue sky as if to make peace,
and it's not what's left of the day's axis or our plans,
or what, besides the catamaran, is missing.
The local airwaves speak of safe spaces,
of finding them and staying put –
rote repetition except for the part
about a short-lived centre, of the wall again,
where the damage tends to be the greatest,
and then the fury on the wall's far side.
We lean on one another, press each other's arms.
The dread at the start of knowing,
waiting on this side

Flying into the Namib Desert

The hooked peak's red layers of outcrop
just under the left wing, surging past
large and closer than surprise as we level off
to where everything borrows the sky –
blue intensity of petrified mud flats,
cloud shadows brimming like ponds and lakes,
pale blue meander of dry streams,
the road a pencilled thought fed by trails,
their grey strung together like stretch bands of sunrise.
A desert sphered for mere dots motionless
yet drifting away in heat waves
edging off the map

We wear our Cessna like a shirt that clings
to back and chest, no room for worries.
Our Parisian pilot smiles, sweat stitching
the privacy of a crease above his lip line.
Ear plugs can't stop the engine's howl,
but deaf for years I know the mouth's curl
of words when he turns his head,
*The sand sea on the horizon ends 80 miles west,
at the Atlantic* his left-hand inching
the steering column to a greater decline,
his right hand compassing a valley
fanning out as though to measure its rising
toward our droning down and coax the moments
of oncoming to pull in on themselves

The surety of marks and motion
oblivious of the sky as concentration
draws attention from the body's every part,
as attention starts to hurry,
as springbok soar like small birds
across the faint direction of landing strip,

Nearness

as the suddenness of cliffs
belays the sun's angle on scrub
and the tall tufts of grass silvering out of the sand

Ostriches stand still: three, four, five of them.
The world levels waist-high
with the recognizable sound and flinch
of wheels on sand. The air sorts out engine surge,
sputter, quiet and the snap of release deep within,
a sudden opening that turns the outside in
with the heat's full-body force;
sand and gravel gather underfoot;
the pilot's nod lures concentration
to all that might still happen

The serpentine indolence wayfaring
on the strip beyond the Cessna's shadow
is a cobra, he says, and he will inform
the warden. Silence
can be distinct as boots printing the sand
or the drum of feet on the boardwalk

An ostrich alone
on the whereabouts of the moment
periscopes high to peer through us
to the other side

Stranger, where are you going?

Nearness

Full Hunter's Moon

The cabin with its eaters of venison,
and the ridgeline's first bloom of release,
darkness separating from itself,
a glow pluming through the silhouette,
a design growing, opening everything
from where I stand,
vague whereabouts finding shapes
in this half-light world

The cabin, the shore,
the cowl of willows
trussed to what's left of the dark
however long I peer that way
just to be sure of movement into the willows,
a buck's stutter steps.
I can be still-bound enough
to squint for high-antlered details.
He stops as though something
is not taken care of,
as though wishing the nonchalance
of the doe's half-truth of shadow to move closer,
waiting for her to turn back,
to refuse the field of light
plausible as the dark, or mountain silhouette,
or moon, or cabin lights out

If I stood like this for an hour or two
I still wouldn't know what the night will bring,
yet it's all I can do to turn away,
the moon climbing through a cloud-lace
shimmer as a shadow immediate as memory
walks me to the door
and vanishes

The Vedder River Run

Rush of current through cloud drift
dark with underwater shudder,
its grammar of terrible need,
dorsal fins rising, sinking back
through green whorls:
humpback salmon upstream.
Migration. Home

This is what I came for back then,
tracking the season's head-on haste:
breath of new snow on Lady Peak and Mount Cheám
and this certainty of passage shifting with the *here*,
strange as dialects feeling their way in our village
of refugees, their mother tongue unsure

Home: shoals where salmon rock grey and white
on their side with the steadiness
of a drowned man's eye into my eyes,
gauntness giving notice like their caudal twitch,
the body loosening death yawns
of the hooked jaw again, again

Home: two eagles stepping forward,
gulls almost holding their own
but lurching aside, keeping back
like the newcomer's standstill of words
waiting for their order and accent
that defined life around us, in us,
that kept the plainness of promises
to a destined place and time,
down to the last gasp,
the final hitch of the tail,
the body's frayed outline

Steelhead Trout

Line screaming out
below the white-water bend despite the brake,
the rod's convulsions in a shore-to-shore shudder,
no slack allowed, arms and back
begging for a final *yes* as it turns our way
with a furious shifting of surface and depth.
Now? Maybe? veering closer, veering,
the question repeated,
a hard jerk into the net

My brother and I
recognize for the first time this holy place,
the knee-down, thigh-down demand,
the net's frantic tessellation of silver,
a suddenness of dorsal sting,
the broad lateral rubescence
like the bleeding finger, eyes firm
with a history from elsewhere caught in the now,
a buck of many ocean runs, not yet spawned out,
its fierce urgency not done with perfection

We find and finger out
the single barbless hook bent half straight.
A quick weigh-in of 29 pounds including
open-and-close gasps large as our hands
which lower him into the shallows

Our stroking his rainbowed flanks
has reasons to ponder how he knows
when he is called to inscribe
his shadow in this river;
but our hands are losing their feeling
for him as we steer his hard hitches
and step sideways toward the deep

Nearness

to follow the thrust of his vanishing
into the current's full force,
into its rows of fractured light breaking out,
slipping past each other,
released from what they were
like the moment's balance
in the river rocks' slickness
as we find our feet, as we turn by inches
into the shift of stones underfoot,
river and shore still watching
what is being taken care of

October Slugs

To let them be
sledding a straight kind of shyness
across the driveway
rough as a gravestone,
tempo its own expectation,
two glistening trails secretly involved
stopping to read their distance to the light
living in the green of vinca minor
and lawn on the other side

A stretch like a swoon
that doesn't know you
as they start again
from where they were —
no this or that,
a future if they can make it,
if they can make it
if they   the distance of time
endless, proposing only itself
in a morning's solemnity

Time as Distance

The moon losing itself in the chalk sky of morning,
fog shoulders the black ridge
of Vedder Mountain beyond the abstract.
A kind of conversation with readiness,
a beginning like recovery
as you close the front door,
find ways around the bulldozed stacks of wreckage
in the cleared land to trails
black-tailing through cedars, cottonwoods,
poplars, willows, quaking aspen,
your lungs heaving less along new cut-riverbanks,
their overhang of soil like a too large hairpiece,
past bars of gravel and sand
and their skeletal estimates of the channel's
hard exchange with what has been

You're back, knowing one day time will eat you alive,
but for now you try to outwalk the fly darting
just ahead like a stubborn floater on the edge
as you leave the woods for the clover's aftermath,
a field cut weeks ago, its green emptiness
pimpled here and there with molehills
greying in the sun now overhead
as if for the first time, your face flushed
as the world around you measures
time as distance, not the way
you've come but as ways of conversation
preceding, following, interrupting,
altering separately, yet of a piece,
the uncommon common —
like the sudden point of mirrored light
from a truck just now barely visible
against the blue of Lady Peak,
and here the hayfield's broad shine

Nearness

narrowed where you stand

Consanguinity

Red whisperings
bleeding into the west end
of Central Road and the prairie,
reaching for something more,
something else, eye-steps
stretching out to meet me
where I'm going:
an evening centuries later,
centuries ago
that wants to understand
a sky serious about common descent
I know too little about.
Bood ties that reach the sun in time
for us to go down together
to earth and deeper still

Hum of Bees

i

Whistle-whir of grey:
two mourning doves the boy
has startled out of a pear tree,
the sky's sharp blue
leaving on wing tips.
In the breathing
stillness, in the wind,
a small shudder, at his feet,
a hum
electric as his father's tuning fork:
turmoil of bumblebees –

he counts to forty
and knows he can count farther –

bees rearranging blossoms,
unhunching small wings,
lifting off and drifting down again
to the lithodora's azure clarity
of stars he can touch,
their narrow gleam

One flower,
one breath,
one bee
under his boot until
the long vibration
of bewilderment
stops

Nearness

ii

If there are moments and places that
like knowing or lack of knowing
need forgiveness, or, like the decades,
forgive themselves, and if memory
is like that, the one remembering will step
well ahead of these words
into the sedge and half-heard
wild-flower drone to the water's edge,
hand shielding his eyes from the sun
and the lake's crewelwork of blue and light
as he follows a barely visible ribbon
of road rising like redemption
from the far shore
into a mountain's sweatered green,
and up to the near world's edge

And here, where he stands,
where summer's indulgence is too full
for words and "even *each other*
doesn't make sense", *
the sway of the grass,
the hum of bees

----

* *Jelaluddin Rumi,*
  "Out beyond ideas of wrongdoing and rightdoing."

Nearness

Pacific Cantos

Nearness

Nearness

Canto 1

Raise an arm in farewell benediction
to the Pacific white from the storm
that made the air and sand more peaceful.
It begins, that yielding up word by word,
the world where you were born.
Some things hold on: spinal curve of a fish skeleton
beside a sand-sequined sneaker pointing landward,
bending the incoming margin of ocean.
A large bird, grey in its wings, standing
in the shoe, wearing it backwards.
Hermit gull looking out to sea,
derelict shoe filling with water,
elfin desolation of bones
run through by eddies

Canto 2

And a long reeling in of the soul,
the feeling of having lost something
important, anthology of purpose
looking for you even after
your return to a green shuffle-down
of the slope, the shoreline's gleam
as the sun sets, night a quarter-moon
roadway streaming like the urgent
hesitation of a touch that stays
a touch away, morning an argument
of small gusts. Salt in the air
and on the lips, your mother tongue again,
the fluency. And millions of years of drift
finding you, weaving currents
through you, this strangeness of being free,
debris left behind like indecision
before a full head of onshore rain

Canto 3

Between the spats of rain
a hymn of sunlight on the surf,
the clouds like Bellini angels on their own.
The line we call horizon does not exist.
Here the peacemakers can say
'more than usual desire, more than usual calm.'
And the patience of the Pacific plate,
that deep-down calculation
which will never allow
that all its ways be told

Canto 4

Years ago, the smell of brown kelp,
the sweet taste of the eel grass,
salt on your cheeks, and in the instant
you turned your back to your three-year-old son,
a rogue wave, emptied lungs, the burn
of sand under eyelids, legs straining
against the pull. "Why didn't you stop it?"
every nerve of his fibrillar body frantic with tremors
despite the change of clothes.
"My clothes hurt." The wonderment.
Learning to give more of himself to matter.
Learning to give more of yourself to fear

Nearness

Canto 5

Far back the Gulf Islands ferry
under a clothesline of clouds
to the margin. Closer in
crescents of black, a pod of orcas,
their purity of motion suspended like moments
in a diorama of time — and the sun lapsing
into itself, setting an ocean on fire.
Wait another hour:
the phantasmal groan of the foghorn
man-hauling the dark's heaviness
from land to sea

Canto 6

Ocean shouldering everything
at dawn where the northern road
ends at Parson's Landing.
The clarity, far out, offers a slow waltz of swells
and the stranded muffle of breakers
forever on the verge of something else.
Rip tides close in to capture desire and doubt,
their struggle against themselves.
You stay where you are, where the shells
of Catalina Island gleam
like fish scales. These leavings,
and a frantic plastic jug
turning only so much, keeping its place,
mouth sucking saltwater and sand
from the tide's longest finger

Canto 7

You remember the Baha images:
two fishermen singing of lovers
and loss, their white and blue
boat double-bowlined to a rock
on the shore, boat and rock becoming a coastline
of an inland sea as you mused
what else the bay held for you
where you could wave the fishermen *adios*
and watch a patch of sea-grass quiver
12 metres down, the wonder of the deep,
how it could lull you into sleep forever

Since you began this canto darkness fell
and the weather turned

Canto 8

The desire before you reached Kailua
Beach, and a promise kept
like the grin for a silly photograph.
The curl of the breakers, thin spray clean
off the top, the upsurge, your body pearling
down into the wave's hollow, arched back
inside the motion, the sea's sudden underbelly
hard beneath you, yourself beached
on the shore, that first breathing groping
spitting after rebirth, chest
bleeding, ears filled with the high surf
percussion, sand rushing back into
the sea, this and a need free of fear,
that will not be satisfied,
drawing you yet again into the offshore
cartwheels

Nearness

Canto 9

Your brother's catamaran seizes the wind
and you seize the harness to hike out, Kailua no more,
the boat urgent, slapping rollers down
and leaping up slopes of swells or plunging
through, the ocean knowing how to whelm
us – a spangled blaze then blue then green
then the reverse and the rush back into light,
wonder riding the edge of grace
into a long trough sinking, unwinding straight,
widening as though to gather the sky's endlessness
and make room for two far-off sails
autonomous, white as miracles,
and the dark shimmer of another notice:
a hammerhead having found us out,
nose touching the tiller, searching for room
in our reverie. "Coming about, brother"

Canto 10

Descend here, eyes ushering you
into a blind world below,
each footstep arranging itself and your senses
down the path's serpentine steepness,
morning fog and flashes of naked light
almost touching the path, and to the right
smallest outbursts of water finding each other
and a spring-fed stream,
sound and light drawing you forward
into absent-mindedness, floating body
and absence, then changing everything
as the fog is winched aside.
There: sword dances of light on a vast
attentiveness of blue
and the stream quietly troughing the sand
to meet it

Canto 11

Ah Victoria, no one forgets your loveliness
riding an island's shoreline like a mirage,
your rookeries of verse hungry
for sea winds, your words winged
for salt marshes filling draining the day,
sometimes the light just so,
sometimes the words keeping their shape
even as cloud shadows unravel
inside the wind's ardour for change,
bringing with it another sky

and yet your underworld fatness
of alimentary canals still spills
all its corruption into the sea.
In the long run an ocean will not negotiate
with your thirdly and fourthly

Canto 12

The ocean's sucking, gasping in the bottlenecked
basalt chamber, a vortex near its mouth
deepening your question of how far,
and no one there to catch you going down,
drowning inside yourself, lungs bursting
to breathe, your eyes still wide, looking
for a sign like the ebbtide,
the chamber emptying, released
from yourself

Canto 13

Rocks in water, water on rocks,
touching them completely, swayer and swayed
under the Milky Way.
We came to this deep-threaded cove
with only the jib up. Small waves
fall quietly into themselves, into evening
steadied by memories: your basso recording
of "Rocked in the Cradle of the Deep,"
children's dreams tousled together in the aft berth,
your wife's clothes one by one unloosed,
drifting down to the floor, readying the night.
An anchorage in the lee of hard winds
and waves across the deck

Canto 14

The dialectic, repetition of change
and change of repetition, the flow of cliffs,
their glow as the sun bends west,
the high-rise rock on Cannon Beach they call
The Haystack, two old men arguing the best way
down to where the shore has undressed
the children, where voices
in the onshore wind measure distance,
where a golden retriever
shakes off an ocean and finds it
yet once again, with joy

Canto 15

This clear look of a drowned fisherman:
a steelhead hen on her side in a shoal
of river rock smooth as bones, final spawning
done. Colours of abandonment,
the onshore haze keeping things as they are,
nothing else for fish or polished stones,
and no need for you and your son,
in camouflage chest waders, to bend down
to gather anything here or to memorize
the dove-hued bracken of her death
or the river's flow
that other steelhead have left
to relearn the salty breath inside
hard northern currents, to bolt down
more than breath and, like the salmon smolt,
work their way against vanishing

Canto 16

In the evening your grandson shivering
in his briefs, a last harelip of light
unaware of you, and he says
you look better with clothes on.
What healing's here for you?
A grandson asleep in your bed,
his dream-twitches keeping you awake,
an ocean washing through you,
the peace of darker darkness you feel
and deeper see, strange
as love rummaging for words

Nearness

Canto 17

Long Beach: other than the end
of a continent, B & Bs, cheap
motels, resorts with 24-hour desks?
In our dreams we are the measured sound
rising from sleep — the muffled tremolo
of surf against the shore, an innermost rhythm
feeling the restlessness in which a shore
defines itself and us sleeping
on its nearness

Canto 18

And awakening to countless sharp-billed
yellowlegs unicycling along the shore,
stopping as one to face the tide, to watch,
to listen, the Pacific still the messenger

Canto 19

There are times when stars are suns
with haloes of fire high above the streetlamps
of Ocean Parkway; there are moments
when you and the fire and the sea
are made for each other and the universes
hum the infinite of time. So many currents
carrying the years

Envoi

This cove's wave after wave falls quietly
into itself, balanced by memory –
an anchorage

Nearness

Nearness

Trees Partly of Wood

The elm in the temple garden
of Takamatsu for 1,200 years,
one living branch left

Nearness

Anniversary of the Lost Boreal Forests

A silence of branches fading,
not even their shimmer remains,
the great water rising over the world
tree by tree, only a bird
riding the surface and shadows trembling
like leaves that must begin their night work,
send their dark down the deepest way
to countless ribs of sunken timbers
half buried, bare stems probing out to meet
the leaves, but the leaves wait only
long enough to start rising, twisting
upward like the dead through all their darkness
to where the bird turns alone
the way the hand of a blind man moves,
the moon scattering the leaves' lightlessness
on melées of driftwood, like the open hinge
of shells the colour of grief

North of Boreality:
Arctic Stencils and Lithographs

Howl of emptiness
lonelier than eyes of the dead,
whiter than the last canoe birch
and last paper birch two days ago.
No trees.
Their absence the no-colour
James Houston leaves untouched
in stone-cuts and sealskin stencils.
If you haven't lived here
it will use up what you've believed,
wherever you are
on Baffin Island.
The air that dropped a veil
has erased the horizon
where dogs vanish harness and all,
the sled following.
Your feet no longer part of you,
or the brief mockery of light,
walk by themselves

At night Houston kept shapes nearby
awake, even the shrieks almost visible
and the moon's moments of milk-eyed blindness
because he knew the time was not yet right
to lie down against the snow-covered confusion
of dogs, a brief of morning bringing pillars of nothing
as if through trees

The four dogs left lead you into Cape Dorset
so they can drop on their haunches
to gnaw frozen blood and white crystals
from their paws, your own chalk feet
blackening in the toes

Nearness

and screaming above your words
to your friend observing closely

When you fly south across the endless fleece
nothing lost comes back to you,
not even something you started to say
as a voice outside you urged *sleep, sleep,*
but when the hospital's off-white
crawls into view,
you know how white has readied itself
for a scrub conifer, and another,
a scattering of them, and more,
inching into their shadows
stencilled in snow
pale as birches

Why Our Town Replaced Silver Maples with Better Trees

i

The buzz of business-and-finance
reminders that *money doesn't grow on trees*
has local support with this difference:
silver maples could be meant
and whatever steps out of their hollowness in ice storms,
or out of softer drumming as the wind kicks up
and the sky clabbers clouds to a jade-green
before it zigzags funnels past the wails of sirens
and unshingles everything

Since the storm you've stood shoulder to shoulder
with trees pieced back together by surgeons,
on the mend now, like your accident-prone neighbour;
or the young women in the county shelter,
including those thrown against walls
with or without a clear view of the door.
These are times when sympathy wants out
like sap through bark,
its rough corrugations resinous,
but you've always been wary of brokenness
and the ways of worrying about it,
how they become a part of you

ii

And so, you've tried not to fret over
the city's silver maples, their canopies gone,
immature firs now reminding the streets
that lamp standards have been recoated pastel blue.
You could complain, but to whom? and why
exactly? You could say the future is what it is.

Nearness

In any case, it's not about to skip town
like the builder and the former mayor,
and the silver maples are not coming back
any more than the pink-skinned for-profit hospital
in the next block, closed a year after opening,
its parking lot a memory board of white lines
shiny as its four-lane entrance to the future
and what's left of the vandalized cyclone fence.
Beyond the fence dust devils carve up the vacancy
where surveyors' stakes left
as suddenly as the hospital's name
and the *fifteen acres for sale* sign

iii

The reasons for walking beyond bankruptcies
and beyond repainted lampposts are ahead of you
where the street ends at a late afternoon field
of hackberry and blue ash shadows –
there, your destination, a smirk remembering,
and not by accident: a polygamous
silver maple. Because you looked quickly,
expecting nothing more than arrival,
arteries quiver like nerves up the early
evening sheen of trunk and lower stems,
the vessels quick with their pulse of blue
as the gust gives way to a trepidation
of late flowers, a fit of leaves and divergent
seed wings. In the sudden dispossession
the bole once again surprises you,
a narrow gash crotch to roots fanning out,
although the crown is round and full.
At your feet everywhere volunteers
in the tangle of vetch and grass, spines gleaming
straight and to the point like a grinning
praise the lord and some of them pushing up
a first fingernail umbrella of leaves

Nearness

iv

And you, standing half in the evening sun
and half in the shade's long reach,
where so much matters,
the way a town freeze-frames its damages,
the bluster of promises,
your walks from one point to another,
the absence of silver maples narrowing streets
like a nave of random shapes and what the mayor called
"their messiness," and here the manifest:
at eye level three antennae of silver-green seedlings
testing the air outside the mouth-shaped cavity
in the trunk like a zany sideway idea,
the tree's deep scar, the vetch and weeds
as high as the volunteers.
And no one to rescue this flagrancy
from itself or a repaved and replanted city
of vacancies, from explanations
less wooden than trees, from the way
this maple saves itself

Graduate Studies

Post-graduate intentions and new marriage ready,
the car's back seat and floor
a helter-skelter of books.
Small bursts of light
in the high-arched naves of trees in Elmwood,
Manitoba, saw us off to qualifying exams
on New England's nostalgia for the future,
how Puritan protocols took command of starting over,
why they timbered trees for a city on the hill,
how a transmigration of divine will
can spread from clearing to clearing
and a fretwork of stumps and burning brush
can make a new world even newer,
even less familiar

Something urgent in our fingertips
as our visas were returned
and we entered America's endless rhythm
of prairie sky, horizon smoking with the dust of harvesters,
and two deer silhouettes stutter-inching
into the red of the setting sun,
the evening confusing distance with hypnotic stare

The next day
throttled down by welcome signs of one-horse-
Budweiser towns, faded block letters
starving for attention,
the white of houses
shadowed by outsized maples and elms,
the sky's blue annexed to their thick heads
as though it is they, the trees,
and not a house or fence that know their place
or a town's gravel lanes or the old man at the last driveway
closing the gate behind him

Nearness

The unschooled part of us hand-signaling
on both sides, waving itinerant towels
in the emptiness of a highway
always setting scenes of trees, at-homeness
of elms recognized in the repetition,
but at the State line's welcome, large trees
splayed in the grass, prone, level with the road
like a decisiveness on the other side of "why,"
and some already stripped and cut clean
into parts like a meat packer's carcass,
Chicago's detours carrying on
where words left off
as we rubbed the last of summer
from bloodshot eyes and found a direct way
beyond the treeless maze and orange cones

The same orange as the cones in front of
Altgeld Hall two weeks after the empty stares
and nodding mostly of registration,
the campus already denuded of its trees,
all elms, only these two left, about to be taken down,
dead and living parts. One tree unsure at first
about this coming down to earth,
the other falling faster as it neared the ground,
storming into silence
as leafy segments shook out their light

When the emptiness stops moving
what is it that remains
where trees once whispered their adjustments?
A brand-new classmate from north of Boston,
the one who left the priesthood, the church and new wife
("nothing has worked out and so I'm here")?
a sky less frugal? the turkey vulture
measuring its time and distance overhead?
the faint smell of sawdust, wind and prairie?
or simply something getting things wrong again?

Nearness

The oldest campus building destitute,
gothic archway too large, chain saws
yellowing the grass like swollen gourds
in the field, and you walk over, bend close,
counting from cambium to the centre,
tallying each tree's life backwards
to the unsure dark of its start,
first count not the same as the next.
But once started, the count continues
and some diseases won't stop.
"Choking off of vessels,"
someone said. "Dutch Elm disease."
And for once I knew the ghostliness in Father,
his tiredness the body's only wisdom,
and he, the priestly drop-out, telling
how the largest elm in town grew
into the basement wall of their undated
colonial house. "Down there in the dark,
when the light switch failed thinking with hands
was easier than finding a flashlight.
And we let those roots stay where they were
long after the tree wilted top-down and died"

There are many ways to tell a tree's life,
even after the tree has gone, and there's
a way an elm will hold light inside of it,
in the early evening turning it to gold

Ice Storm

It was more than the kind of shift in seasons
that sets off warnings of weather fronts
running across the screen in disagreements:
the horizon too narrow
for the largest tree in our neighbourhood
caught in a silver thaw's dead-of-night explosions,
an all-around staccato, and then
a world crashing down
close to where we lay awake

We could argue who screamed first
and leapt out of bed to find candles
and who made the first flashlight stabs
into the night where it was closest,
but that wouldn't change
the early morning's breakdown:
sky open and our hackberry tree's
one-way message laid out four ways,
a hundred-foot section
partly out of the picture
lodged inside the neighbour's bedroom,
another part like a question
pounded through the modest linears
of our detached garage,
and two parts of tree and ice shards
massed across the powerline
and fences side and back,
measurements no longer suitable,
nor years we had counted on
or the steel-cabled tracery
to hold the tree's inner life together

(these lines will outlast you and your tree)

Nearness

Sometimes a poem is removed
from those that hold together
because it is closer to something else:
dying as a situation that is no more
but brings with it sounds of an end
and words searching what is left . . .

A tree of one hundred twenty-nine rings
and almost entirely of wood

Don't Ask

how loyalty leaves an opening for the earthmover,
or where the garden was, what happened
to cherries, Mirabelle plums and pears
that watched the sky etch scribbles of branch
and leaf shadows on the evening wall
before they deferred to the dark

Don't ask how newest leaves could be so serious
about shivering, their skin luminous as the night
or how young sprigs brushed against sleep
like a warm hand marking endlessness,
or whether the morning burdened a bough
until the fruit weighed down
to the overspread of grass and chickweed
greening the dry season

Don't ask why a moment's balance of finger
and thumb held a close-up of two
cherry stems almost in the middle;
how the air assumed the fragrance and gestures of plenty,
dusting each plum in a sweet revel of ripeness;
why a small red intemperance
brushed the Mirabelle's gold
after you decided to wait another day
for the pear's perfection, radiant as a kiss
stolen from the soft flesh of God

Nearness

The Yellow Transparent Apple Tree

The tree stands under a patch of sky
that overlooks our lives
unlike the eternal orchards of the Louvre,
their apples, hand-shaped perfectly
by dream sparks in the garden's green,
smooth as Eve's full breasts

The summer I learned to read
Father photographed our apple tree,
twice as tall as I in my sailor suit.
You can't see the sheen
of the oozing fracture at the first branch,
but you can see the bole's thinness
and the small shade on the boy's bare feet
before he steps out of the picture
to go inside the blue and white house
to open the case of the quarter-size violin
on his father's bottom shelf
and practice open strings and simple scales;
the old newspaper lining the shelf
distracting him, headline bleeding black
and a havoc of smaller words,
some of which are real to him,
"600 sailors lost" above a ship darkened by water

The boy sees a hull cut into equal halves,
and sailors rising like apples,
the surface gathering them,
three and four at a time
the way he held the spindly tree's
first-year apples against his chest,
carried them up the steps
onto the porch, laid them out
on the table until there were no more

Nearness

I'm walking with my son, a head taller than I,
into evening between sun and house,
past apple crescents
drying on cotton-white racks
to where fragrance of ripe apples
clings to the air

A slight touch of the boot
against a large apple split full length,
the flesh swollen white
in the crush of shadow and grass

And all around a litter of golden apples
bruised by small sharp moments of light

Pink Dogwood

> *"the pink lungs of their bodies*
> *enter the fire of the world*
> *and stand there shining"*
>   Mary Oliver, "Moccasin Flowers"

A certain order sudden as the season
teaching us to number our days:
first, a smallness of dried-blood petals
buckled to a grimace like autumn leaves

And yet a fixed image has poorer odds here
than a hard frost because it's become an idea,
even as the petals open themselves like wings
with a natural grace of nakedness,
radiant around a subtle centre
too cramped for notice
in the flesh-coloured translucence
barely breathing at dawn against the ivied wall

Fastidious surplus within colour.
Squint at the thousand petals enflamed by the sun,
this is now, not absence,
conferring privilege on itself,
a luminous blush of days on end
reaching out to margins of light
as if to hold them there for greater sheerness
and the moment by moment rhythm of leaf starts

Words, like theories,
can get in front of everything,
despite small and large and gain and loss
still refusing to reconcile.
But when the heat wave's skittishness
wakes the light an hour

Nearness

before anyone inside is aroused
by the flash of sun,
the sound you heard
in your deep sleep
was the wind on the season's heels
redesigning the tree, the colour's excess

and the hue itself like a trope
for bracts of blossoms
brown as wrinkled parchment
on the ground bark put down two weeks ago,
memory unready with what happened,
but letting it pass into what is not
and what is:
an unfamiliar softness of leaves
unravelling like summer,
the ovate emerald of every leaf,
its slight fold tipped upward at the point
as if to defer a ghostly underside to the sun

even as a tree of pink blossoms
has pressed itself into sharp relief,
almost a way of looking at the world,
refusing to leave the mind alone
as clouds ride at ease
on the long back of time

Nearness

Birches of Lake Winnipeg

> *I have heard of a man in Maine who copied*
> *the whole Bible on to birch bark. It was so*
> *much easier than to write that sentence which*
> *the birch tree stands for.* H.D. Thoreau, Journal

Check wind ripples in the small rollers
groping toward you
without fuss out of the dark.
Grasp the gunnels evenly,
step inside with the left leg almost centred,
knee below chin, push off
the right leg balanced on a moment
like something just remembered,
then in, wet to the knees –
you're always talking about white trees,
how you swam beneath them
that night as meteors crisscrossed the sky
toward the sea –
securities of the abstract trailing off behind,
the canoe braiding water
into sunrise, into rollers reddening,
slapping the bow. The horizon
an endless sweep of light
igniting the sea with every other breath

i

You glance away, you glance back.
Whiteness, a margin for land and water
awakened as one, indistinguishable
except for the dark between trees,
two groves leaning out to face
the sun's first light, silver trumpets
glossed with calm hysteria

Nearness

on the shore of the world,
the canoe birches spotless
stems whiter than white birch,
the dull gold of August kindled like desire,
burning its way to the top until
it flames above black spruce

ii

A canoe will grow smaller, outside in,
on the sea-road of the Canadian Shield
as arms and hands work with water
through the broken cadences of light

You are here,
nowhere important;
that's your reward,
the hours easing the sun westward,
the shore like a smirch on a mirror,
but each moment of horizon
truer than the last, nudging you on
until the birches are your markers again,
tops forked in twos and threes,
and forest-line north and south
in endless deference

The shore praying over shadows
and small stones,
sand breathing, sucking
under the rocks' black cape
as you beach, the birches separate
as on Thoreau's north-side hill
where their white centred him
as he sent surveyor lines, wordless,
into woods, trued old stakes
and drove new markers firmly down

Nearness

iii

In the evening, the birches darken
to bronze at the ground
and ruddy copper at the waist
before unbuttoning their white
higher up, full length of ravelling,
inner bark red as blood,
fresh sap on the bark smooth to the lips,
almost sweet, dried sap
the shade of the goldeye's stare
before the fish is smoked;
trees wrapped in the moon's
slow voyage until they're whole again,
even the graceless notion of stump,
its beavered pyramid ghostly
with planes and grooves and light

iv

There's no path to birches,
only morning criss-cross,
vague whereabouts
and deer trail whispers.
So, you start with what's ahead helping you
as the wind lifts a blackbird's wings
a few feathers at a time.
You stop, not for its song but to wait
until your lashed eye is calm again,
the body a kind of rival leaning forward
to continue, soul leaning to the side,
the sudden joy of being scolded by jays

The intrigue of having come full circle
and no birches — but there, the small clearing,
last evening's unfinished map
of what you knew,

Nearness

and a tree before you diffusing light
like newspaper in the sun,
small prints rolled back on the trunk

This too is news.
A tree unscrolling
when no one was watching,
bark beginning to spool the other way,
starting again near the cambium,
its flesh inured by another day

Coming out differently
on the fateful slope to the season's end

Words and Tree

The pilgrim sky watches you outwait the night
in the place you have made
under the fruitless cherry tree

You have chosen this tree,
you know its name,
and when the smallest moments
of morning arrive like rain
you shake off the chill and greet the day

The tree presses your back, you feel its pulse.
Some of its leaves hide birds
and sometimes a leaf falls soundlessly
like blossoms when a bird flies out
over the shade's edge

There is something more you know
about this tree,
more than its humming quiet
or its thickly forested head
or the missing limb that will not re-grow
like the lizard's tail,
or the tree's refusal to change
when its name was changed by the villagers.
You will not say even to yourself
what it is you know. You wait
like the words, like the leaf
and its brown petiole in your hand

        * *

All those days and nights the banyan's
hundred arms prayed themselves
back into the earth, to rootedness

Nearness

that held you the way light is held
by an evening of water caught in a lapse
of time that does not want to end.
"The time of words is over" Bonhoeffer wrote,
but it will come again and again
like the banyan's new starts
fingering the ground's barrenness.
The words will come

* *

All this time you've lived with trees
certain of their place,
trees that outlive the fury of extremes,
like the cedar of a thousand years
not far from your home
to which you've returned, to the solitude
urging upward inside
the cedar's phloem and cambium
to the highest stem, then earthward
as newness, as the outside congealing
another ring, imperfect circle
round the last, closing like seasons.
A small bird on the lowest branch
grooms itself in hurried bursts
and so, you keep still,
praying the words further inward
from the red sheen to the xylem
and heartwood dark with time

No answer,
no choosing

Only words and tree,
the quiet of consent

Nearness

Cantos of Oak

Nearness

Cantos of Oak

There are always books to choose from
but for the third time book towers hoard the floor,
books that moved with you across continents

You've pulled markers from new-jacket volumes
you didn't know you had
and old folios repaired. You box them
with former standard editions recognizable
by their always near-green spines.
It's time for you to see this through.
These books tell what *lifetime* is
if not divestiture or what you mean
with a simple good-bye after you bartered them
for a friend's seamless bookcases
finished last week, taller than you
when they lean back. Perfect posture,
the grain of the patterns agreeing
and disagreeing, some almost vertical
like moonlight on water, some with groined arches
like a nave, or an arabesque confusion,
many jaggedly sure of their rising and falling lines
like a healthy EKG

You don't even have to say oak,
and you don't have to leave the centre of the room
to name the species –
one of eighty oaks of North America.
The name will sound intended

At night you check off trees again
but not the books – at the edge of your half sleep
a large bottle leaning against hot coals,
fills with smoke, and you seem to remember
a forest like black mangroves on a mangle of nothing,

Nearness

no branches reaching down into porous grey
to what is silent and yet
new roots and trunks and a long moan

Awakened by the wind, you know
if leaves are sweeping the street bare
or shattering the air like a thousand birds
startled away to hidden places,
one by one the leaves will find themselves,
find each other, find a broad way
back to your yard, a new squall-line's
avant-garde

       You brook the spell
of sitting up and dropping bare feet
less than an inch above the hardwood floor
about to take your breath away, to exchange it
with the wind's provocations.
You're thinking branches again,
their frantic black against the night,
unsevered like petioles holding in the gusts

The feet know how many steps to the corridor
even if you stop to listen.
The ceiling light
surprises the blond of polished stairs,
balusters and rail down to the door –
pushed hard.
From the dark of the land
a long fringe of oaks
travelling slowly eastward, westward,
stopping only to gather their silhouettes
of hunched heads

Nearness

Canto 1

A book that gets you out, that crosses roads,
paths, clear-cuts, tangles of endless underbrush,
garbage, and animal turds, meets a wind
sure about direction to a particular tree
belonging mainly to an unmapped sky:
that's one of the books you keep.
Forty-six live oaks have made
the *List of Famous and Historic Trees*.
The live oak, heaviest hardwood
of North America, tapping down like nerves
through the red earth smell of the South,
medium sized between the half-painted
put-down of grocery store and glitzy new motel,
but one of the largest oaks when alone,
like the two with full moss beards greying
twenty miles north of Boggy Bayou
if you take the local road

Whitman's solitary tree,
that made him think of himself,
generous host for every kind of life,
bark furrowed into ruddy plates, its fruit
abundant, wild, unforgettable to the tongue,
March dying back into a diorama of unfolding grace,
oblong leaves utterly private,
their margins entire, loyalty the year round

This morning no other trees were near
and the oaks waited
like the unfinished clouds above them
riding at ease, thunder over the Gulf,
barely audible, yet birds rising as one
and vanishing northward
as gusts mowed a cloud shadow in the grass.
Driving north in the sudden dark,

you're shouting to yourself
"by itself poetry hasn't improved anything,"
but a live oak can fill loneliness like a hymn.
Even the greatest, most gregarious bard,
who wrote Emerson of rootedness
in the new world, in its largest cities,
broke off a branch, placed it in full sight
on his writing table, thinking of a book
he would write someday, songs of how the life
inside us, around us, might fit inside words,
a green oak branch laid across his page,
larger than the page. Walk over: touch the leaves,
touch the stem end again – lightly.
Twig and mercy. Mercy and tree.
Solitary live oak, the land awakening,
growing large with congealed light and haze
behind the storm's dark veil

Canto 2

Always defeat conspiring with the victors
and the museum's arguments over what to choose
out of shouts and chants from the high rock face
now quiet as the oaks and the cropped commons
of Harrison and the Prophet's battleground,
the years still watching, knowing
how a day's madness can cross its own tracks
yet again, how an evening sun
separates the living from the dead
and the markers from a litter of acorns
naked as corpses, many hidden by others,
by burdock and the collapse of grass

Choose a nut still in its woody cupule,
put its almost perfect roundness
between your lips and teeth

to tease the shell into a soft release of flesh
stinging the tongue with a black ink
bitterness. It will humble you

Canto 3

A thought last evening felt in the arms,
an urge to move the house closer to the trees.
But not before I cut all the way
through a red oak's stricken reckonings
as I promised, days back, when the tree
bloodied and jammed the saw
with the tight squeeze of everything it has been,
picked the chain clean away,
left whatever red remained
to late winter storms and their bare snaps
blunt as a trigger when my father sighted the sky
without a bullet

Today a morning of coots and mergansers
overhead and the whomp of the world
to meet the tree without ceremony,
the rain quiet where the tree now lies
pointing north, away from the house.
I count more than two hundred rings,
no year the same, some so pinched
they borrow themselves from the last or coming one,
and here a year of large growth:
winter mild, summer cool
and wet as the croak of the blue heron
looking past all that is there, its belly full.
The sap on my fingers
neither bitter nor sweet

Untold rings of solicitude
for the next year, a future counted on,

bachelor uncles for years that did not end
in barrenness, guardian rings embraced
by many more

Canto 4

No one will beg loyalty from scrub oak
north of what we've known or from black gumbo
and club-roots bulldozed house-high
in Selkirk's newest suburb-to-be,
but beyond this wreckage of a spent summer
our minds are full of purpose

For hours we followed a trail,
the low narrow kind of white-tailed deer,
thinking grassy clearing, shivering
a moment where the way intersects
with fresh hoof marks among leaves
already the rumpled grey of the earth

Around us middle-earth shapes,
dwarf bur oaks of Manitoba twice as high
as Minnesota corn, furrowed trunks
thin and brown as our children's arms
that point to where this trail and others meeting it
lose themselves in an open space
in which we stand tall as the length of our shadows,
posted on each other.
We're strangers here among fugitive tracks,
we stay with them, with each other,
trace a way toward the turn
that will find our way back by dark

At night the children arc themselves
as though they'd stretch across an evening
on any floor just to hear us tell of oak leaves

Nearness

that won't let go of branches when the snows begin,
how spring returns and each tree's slenderness
stands in the centre of a place grown large
with the dark of pools, how even then
leaves stay on like voices calling each other,
echoes starting inward,
going farther, growing quiet

Our words simple. We tell the children
not to go into these woods alone

Canto 5

A pin oak next to the stop sign
summons your street, but no one mentions it.
Still, there's that moment of bare feet in boots,
the brash green and a sudden angle
that can't tell if branches really reach the ground,
or which is lobed leaf, which are the bristle-pointed teeth,
which are sinuses, which is light

But when the sudden quickness
of the May wind passes through your willingness
to stay with what is here,
most of last year's leaves are sent earthward
to become more precise among skinny leaf shapes
of deep indentations already etched
on the concrete walk, tea-rubbed lithographs.
Step through the leaves, turn them slowly
with the toe of your boot: petioles will shrink
like worms found out too suddenly,
touched too hard

Canto 6

Cloud smudge and flame-blackened pitch pines.
Below a bone-dry brief of earth, shale,
and sugar sand that didn't choose any
of a summer burn's black and white considerations
or a lone jay's ceremonies of complaints
in New Jersey's pine barrens

Wince of recognition. I pick a stem
of dust-enameled scars round as half-moon
ladder rungs instead of leaves, a sprout amputee
with a small shining stranded at the woolly tip,
purplish terminal, not yet dead
and larger than three lateral buds
clustered where the terminal begins.
Lower down two small buds born to die like promises
trying to come back by themselves
from the great fire like the obsequious fox
on scorched feet.
Not summer, not fire, not rain, not ash
nor earth pulling at my boot soles;
it's the severed sprig
that has brought me to my knees,
and when I whirl it over my shoulder
I hear the sound of nothing, how it folds away
where soil runnels into a seared world's lifelines

The sky favouring a slight impatience of rain
as I look down again – a bear oak sprout
beside me, less than a metre high,
five buds ruddy and full,
and under the reach of a barberry bush
a seedling small as a name inside a breath

> *How to help a young oak*
> *as it struggles with our words?*

Nearness

Forest preserves are countries not of their own
but of an uncertified world around them,
and there once was forest here with tracks
of needle-strewn bark and oak-leaf mulch

How far to go where the rain leaks
into every part of the afternoon,
into the light from nowhere, into the barrenness?

The way back darkened by charred scent-post,
widow-makers, re-sprouting boles and timbers
strewn like lines of indecision

Then the simple revelation of firebreak,
of forest again, its legend of miles

Canto 7

In central Indiana mid-summer
sticks to you, nothing else for it to do
than witness your life, even your standstill
as she straightens to greet you,
hat-scarf at her feet. She's flying to Brazil
to visit her former symphony director,
a simple arrangement like her straw hat
top-down on the other side of the yard
under the scarlet oak that whets the shade
of her white Georgian house

Sometimes a tree in a myrtle bed
flowering pale indigo is immense
like hers between the root-buckled walk
and small porch that seem to ask
"what if you'd lived here all your life?"
The hat filled with weeds

Nearness

Perhaps it's that Lorraine considers loss
a delicate gesture,
even the emailed message
on her seventy-third birthday
from the new conductor
who leaps to the podium with his resumé
of good looks and high-hand salute –
he's trimming the strings and increasing
the brass: the violins will not need her

Although heart-rot damage is visible
where the lowest limb had let go
as though no longer part of a plan,
Lorraine's oak stands straight, inner bark
red as a hat-scarf in place.
No matter whether the storm
has been foreseen or not,
and whether doors and shutters
are tightly closed,
a scarlet oak will not bend,
but it will let you know
how wrong you've been

On Salisbury Street
screech owls nest
in the crown of her tree
sheared off by last winter's ice,
and despite a lifetime of trust
or a moment of grace in a day's swelter
a branch will break.
One day the tree will break

Canto 8

The rumble of white oaks unloading at the mill,
the man on the dock's far end
reading them like a document, watching for burls,
spherical tumours over injury
that grow fast on stems, defying the host,
healing over irritation with their own
wild finery of grain
darker than the heartwood's

Their price is figured separately
from the ordinary column stacked
until ready for the rattle, nasal whine
and full throat scream of the ripsaw,
where men size up stripped longitudinals
screaking past, paler than the gloves
of the men stepping edgeways
through shafts of light, gloves that seem to signal
each other. The men do not look up

If you're unacquainted with ripsaws
you can use fingers as earplugs
to dull down the distress
as you watch something more familiar –
hands, for instance,
how they find the insides of gloves
like a quick glance
that doesn't need explanation,
but you will want the men to explain
why they start a day's rhythm
with finger-drumming
that waits for the saw
to cut the log broadside clean,
your own fingers curling like a pianist's
for the cadence
just as the next log rises high,

half upright, wide end crashing down
before the dead whack of narrower end,
the saw's abrupt quiet, the shouts,
and you startled by the silence
of manic movement,
by the log's white bowels,
by the pallets' shine to the top
and the overthrow on the floor

Canto 9

This you know:
there are places you can return to that are faithful,
and the Fraser Valley seems intended,
mostly green like the morning sheen
of wetlands and cedars
Volkert Vedder preempted when he soured
on the gold rush in the Cariboo

The frugality of his son's journal
didn't blame neighbours or an angry god
for a father's mistakes or his own
but roamed like his dog's nose-down back-and-forth
through the fields, half-empty pages
noting how the weather's impatience
could ruin a week, how much wider the stream
his father named after himself had grown,
how few the oaks among the trees
away from the water

You still love this place,
its bugle shape imagined more than once,
ice-age rivers venting their fine grain
toward the sea to change almost everything again,
take parts away and leave others
as though loss, like gain, is a form of sharing.

Nearness

Here the sky comes from more than one direction,
yet summer visitors think daylight
and the forests are forever

Horseshoe ring of mountains hung
just over valley flats,
and Sumas Mountain afloat on berry fields
like the improbable blue of a cargo ship
through orchards on the Welland Canal

Fields fenced for purpose, streams restless,
and all the trees partly of wood.
When they begin to die, they are mostly wood,
like the Oregon white oak beyond the railroad bridge,
almost lost in the surface fog of the river,
but dreaming out of the mist,
growing familiar, looking straight this way,
ricochet of sun on its full and withered stems,
former channel below the tree
settled with river rock, sand,
loose folds of grass and uncertain morning
where you print your way step by step

At the shade's darkest edge
a Steller's jay listens past his good-looking crest,
patient as the smoothness of root ends near the shore.
He cracks an acorn, draws out its emptiness,
gathers himself up into the tree
awakened by a sharp breeze,
by the living and dead stems' start-and-stop,
the austerity – solitary oak
where a continent's western slope
first and last still rises.
You're not needed here

There may be spirits in an old oak
like the spirit-nerves in us,

Nearness

alive as cloud caravans finding each other,
streaming eastward

The rain near, and neither the tree
nor your words will stop the sudden gusts.
But you can step inside the tree's vanished shade
to its bole, and you do, the rise and fall of sound
almost like the river's, the bark's naked ridges
dividing ancient grey and brown

Stop, touch with your palms,
whisper your eyes higher:
an entire tree your only idea, the jay gone.
No need to hurry the small shatter of leaves
that turns your head, that you trust

A remote shiver that has taken years,
this not being needed,
this being together

Author Profile:

Leonard Neufeldt graduated summa cum laude from Waterloo Lutheran University (Wilfred Laurier) and received his MA and Ph.D in the USA. He was appointed Professor of American Studies at Purdue University in 1978. He and his wife have spent most of their professional years in America and abroad, notably in Europe and Turkey. Lecture tours have taken him to India (twice), Germany, Korea and China. "Rootless lives may be as endemic to the Canadian and American West as root-bound ones," he laments, "but in a world of change, there is little defense for either condition."

Neufeldt's scholarly essays and books have appeared with Cambridge University Press, Oxford University Press and Princeton University Press, among others. More recently his seventh book of poetry, *Painting Over Sketches of Anatolia* (Signature 2015), reflects life in both Turkey and coastal B.C. Neufeldt's poetry considers revolutions, wars, the Holocaust, obsolete belief systems, the power of individual and cultural memory, language as social process, the limits of language, and, not least, our life in and with nature.

www.ingramcontent.com/pod-product-compliance
Lightning Source LLC
Chambersburg PA
CBHW070942080526
44589CB00013B/1613